Picturing the Prairie

Picturing the Prairie

A Vision of Restoration

Philip Juras

Foreword by Hank Paulson

Essay by Stephen Packard

LITTLE BLUESTEM PRESS

Little Bluestem Press
Athens, Georgia

Design by Janice Shay/Pinafore Press
Maps by Brad Sanders

Library of Congress Control Number: 2021904900

ISBN 978-0-578-86458-7

Printed in Canada

bobolink
FOUNDATION

To those whose efforts allow us all to imagine what was,
experience what is, and envision what can become
of the tallgrass prairie ecosystem.

Contents

FOREWORD

I have never known anyone quite like Philip Juras. Yes, he is a gifted landscape artist. He is also a superb botanist, historian, writer, and speaker. He plunges into the landscapes he paints, immersing himself in their botanic identity and composition, the human and geologic history behind them, and their moods in different light and weather, always striving to convey the power and beauty—as well as the specific character—a particular scene holds for him. I've long admired individuals who I consider "best in class." Philip has firm footing on that list.

Philip's greatest gift, however, is helping me—and others—to more fully see and appreciate landscapes that I thought I knew. His paintings capture an Illinois documented by early travelers, but fragmented and transformed over the decades and difficult to imagine now. The paintings stand as testimonials to the magic and magnificence of landscapes unique to our region, and whose true value I did not really understand until I saw them through his art.

I grew up next to Spring Creek Prairie, an ancient gravel hill prairie that is part of Cook County's Spring Creek Forest Preserve. Its historical and ecological significance was lost on me until my wife Wendy and I moved back to Illinois—to the very place I grew up—nearly fifty years ago. Wendy befriended local ecologists who taught her about the prairie landscape native to this region, including the grasses and forbs unique to it, and encouraged her to become involved in local efforts to restore and rebuild this largely vanished ecosystem. I was supportive and intrigued by the rarity of the landscape and even participated in the efforts to reclaim it, helping to gather seeds from native plants and clear invasive species. And I was impressed by the transformation from degraded or destroyed sites to ones thriving with a diversity of plants and wildlife.

In the ensuing years, Wendy discovered an artist in Georgia—Philip Juras—who had completed a large collection of paintings that depicted the re-imagined landscapes described by William Bartram, a Revolutionary-era naturalist who traveled in the Southeast and documented his exploration in the classic book, Bartram's *Travels*. Philip subsequently produced more than five dozen paintings of the live oak forest, pinewoods, salt marshes, and dunescapes of a Georgia barrier island that were featured in two major exhibits.

As we came to know Philip better, it was clear that he had a deep interest in grasslands of all kinds. Wendy invited him to Illinois in 2013, and introduced him to a few local grassland restorations and the people who worked in them. Philip was hooked. Again, he painted and produced a body of work over several years that, quite frankly, takes our breath away.

As he had done with the landscapes of Bartram and of the Georgia barrier island, Philip dove into the history and ecology of the sites he visited. He explored them from before dawn until after dusk. He got to know restoration leaders, participated in workdays, and helped with—and painted—prescribed burns. He compiled a list of prairie remnants around the state, devised routes to visit as many as he could, and made multiple trips to Illinois from his native Georgia, in a van packed with food, camping equipment, easel and paints, and his bike. In a few brief years he had visited and come to know deeply more remnant native prairies and savannas than we had even heard of, much less seen.

This book represents the fruit of Philip Juras's Illinois prairie pilgrimage. Pausing over the images—some of which, happily, hang on our walls—I cannot help but consider how much we Illinoisans had missed: more than 99% of these uniquely midwestern grassland landscapes had been degraded by neglect, or destroyed by development and agriculture. At the same time I am deeply grateful for the work of dedicated restoration volunteers and professionals who continue to bring many sites back to their native character. I'm equally grateful for Philip's paintings, which communicate and celebrate both re-imagined grassland landscapes and ones well on their way to healthy restoration. They open my eyes to the very special beauty of the Prairie State, and invite me to pay more attention to it, value it, and work harder to conserve and restore it.

I hope and trust that they will do the same for you.

Hank Paulson
Barrington, Illinois

Tallgrass Roots and the Culture of a New People

by Stephen Packard

Philip Juras and I share a need and a hope. Like Philip, when I stand in a scrap of ancient prairie, I'm transfixed by the colors, sounds, and complexity around me. I hear a Henslow's sparrow sing from its perch on a bearded wheat grass. I see a regal fritillary sip nectar from a Sullivant's milkweed. In this landscape, we sense the past and at the same time feel the thrill that we humans at long last have begun to recognize these ecosystems for the treasures they are.

Thinking I came for beauty and revery, soon I find myself pulling invasive white sweet clover. The prairies now need us; they need invasive-weed pulling. They need our reverence, they need paintings; they need us to share the vision that people and nature can have a rich future together.

The Old World retains nothing like these ecological gems; in Europe, original nature on rich soils was long ago replaced by cultivation and habitation. Here in the New World, dense farming spread through nature at the same time that universities were being founded. In this way,

starting in the late 1800s, scientists began to study the biosphere and soon visionaries realized that we are stewards of ancient, vulnerable, complex ecosystems.

Through a series of publications beginning in 1898, Henry Cowles at the University of Chicago helped define for the world what an ecosystem is and how it functions. His students and other Illinoisans recognized that we were losing our last original ecosystems and, just in time, started the long process of creating institutions to save what remained. It began to dawn on some that we people are now crucial to the survival of the biodiversity of our planet. Learning and taking initiative remain crucial to this day. Thus this book came to be.

In 1937, the eco-prophet Aldo Leopold wrote, "Our ability to perceive quality in nature begins, as in art, with the pretty. It expands through successive stages of the beautiful to values as yet uncaptured by language."

But culture, values, aesthetics, and ethics develop slowly. In 1957, May T. Watts of the Morton Arboretum published *Reading the Landscape: An Adventure in Ecology,* about midwestern wetlands, farms, prairies, and woods. By popular demand, she would later write *Reading the Landscape of America* and *Reading the Landscape of Europe.* In her important work, awareness of principles that the world sorely needed were beginning to emerge. But when Watts celebrated nature, it was not the lonely, introverted nature of Thoreau. It was a nature of people and participation. In 1958, Watts penned a prophetic letter to her student, Barbara Turner, thanking her for a tour of "a neighborhood woods" in Long Grove, Illinois. Watts wrote Turner:

> *What a memorable afternoon… Yours is the sort of community that one meets in books but seldom in real life. It is good to see you bound together by woods and a stream and rolling hills and a common interest in these things, rather than by roads, and telephones and committees. We enjoyed every minute, from the fire and sherry to the last look at your birds and hills and homes.*

Turner would later donate her part of that high-quality oak woodland to The Nature Conservancy, which was coming into existence at the same time. The Conservancy would in time permanently dedicate it into the Illinois Nature Preserves System (which did not then yet exist). These two women were leaders in the building of conservation culture. These were not the "environmentalists" who protested pollution, or chained themselves to trees. They would come later, after Rachel Carson's *Silent Spring* was published in 1962, and were much needed at that time. But Turner and Watts already had a longer view of a community of appreciation and support for natural ecosystems that, to be successful, must be rewarding enough to grow sustainably, from generation to generation.

In 1972, Northeastern Illinois University professor Robert F. Betz published a nine-page essay under the humble title "What is a Prairie?" He knew that he had to start with the basics; both the tallgrass prairie and the concept of an ecosystem needed to be generally understood.

Dr. Betz pointed out that the word "prairie" did not refer to vacant lots between houses (as he had heard the word used throughout his childhood). It did not, he wrote, refer to a cow pasture, or "the open land of our western states." He described the prairie's rarity, complexity, and beauty, but his words would have made little impact by themselves. When they appeared in a book of photographs, *The Prairie: Swell and Swale* by photographer Torkel Korling, they took on a new power. The book's sixty-four pages of exquisite full-page, jewel-like photographic portraits stunned me and many others, especially when Betz pointed out that the last few prairie remnants were still being lost. It would, he warned, be "immoral to destroy… the biological world from which mankind arose." Thus began what Betz and others referred to as "Prairie Fever."

Fevers, fads, and "all-the-rage" moments may contribute to culture, but the last prairies were still, one by one, passing into oblivion. Yet midwestern conservationists were about to take a series of big steps that would influence people around the world.

In the 1950s, George Fell, a private citizen from Rockford, raised hue and cry among the few ready to listen, calling for action. Nationally, he organized The Nature Conservancy, destined to become a planetary exemplar and powerhouse of natural land acquisition. At home, he organized an approach, soon to be copied by state after state,

to save the little fragments of prairie, one by one. The best surviving remnants were to be found in few-acre patches along railroad rights-of-way and in semi-abandoned settler cemeteries, where they had been long ignored; now they were being noticed.

Birth of a Collaboration

There were not remotely enough resources to do what was needed in any single agency, so Fell devised a private/public collaboration that included governments at all levels. His Illinois Nature Preserves System initially had few resources and no staff. But the 1963 Illinois Natural Areas Preservation Act allowed any person, corporation, or agency to dedicate rare, high-quality ecosystems, which then would be permanently protected by state government from development, roads, or any kind of human destruction. The idea caught on. People, villages, and park districts began enrolling their most precious properties. To run this effort, Fell established the Natural Land Institute and raised funds and hired staff.

Another huge step was taken in the 1970s with the creation of the Illinois Natural Areas Inventory, a first-of-its-kind effort to survey the whole state and discover where those last remnants of nature survived. It identified 610 prairies, fens, bogs, woods, and ponds. We learned that 7/100ths of 1% of the state survived as relatively untouched nature. All the rest was cornfields, strip mines, cities, and degraded wildlands. Of the prairie, we learned, less than 1/100th of 1% survived.

By 1978, the Nature Preserves System included sixty-eight preserves, owned by eighteen agencies, including three tallgrass prairies, and it permanently protected 17,149.5 acres from ecological degradation. Fewer than ten of those revered acres were black-soil prairie.

I somehow learned of these developments by reading obscure Nature Preserves "Two-year Reports" and the Betz and Korling book. I began to devote every spare hour to prairie volunteering. Then, almost miraculously, I was awarded my life's first honorable full-time job by the Illinois Nature Preserves Commission. I started saving and restoring remnants, which is how I met Barbara Turner and her woods.

There was at that time no "savanna fever" or "oak woodland fever," but the Inventory did an outstanding job of articulating prairie preservation priorities, in part because of decades of creative study by Dr. Betz. (It did less well on the conservation of oak savannas and woodlands,

the other major Illinois ecosystems.)

When I first encountered Barbara Turner's precious Nature Preserve woodland, I was disappointed. When I asked her to show me some of its rare plants, she couldn't find them. It puzzled and disturbed her; but she was happy that someone cared. In time we would find that Turner's woods needed restoration. It needed people and new principles. But they would not come quickly.

Early clues had emerged in the 1940s, when Aldo Leopold and his colleagues at the University of Wisconsin were asked to advise on the creation of an arboretum. Rather than adopting the standard practice–bringing in tree species from around the world–the Madison folks decided to restore regional ecosystems. In the early years, all their planting attempts failed to thrive. But in the case of the prairie, someone ultimately decided to violate principles of the day by burning it.

The dramatic surge of quality in what soon became recognized as the world's first ecosystem restoration by means of fire was analyzed in scientific journals, and its fires dramatized in Walt Disney's documentary *The Vanishing Prairie*. When Betz later searched for and discovered nearly invisible remnant prairie plants in the mowed lawns of old cemeteries, he used science and the Disney film to convince local cemetery association boards to stop mowing and allow him to burn there. These little remnant prairies then visibly recovered diversity and health.

Initially, the Illinois Nature Preserves System sought to protect land from people. No hunting, no fishing, no timber harvesting; no gathering of mushrooms, berries, nuts, or anything; the principle was: "We've destroyed almost everything! Leave it alone!" But for the prairies—after great debate described later by Betz as bitter and painful in the extreme—approval was given to burn. Knowledge and minds were evolving.

Discovering What Nature Needs

During this time, a few of us noticed that high-quality oak savannas and woodlands were losing acreage and quality, much like the prairies. When we cautiously burned the wooded edges of the prairies, we saw biodiversity recovering there too. I remembered Barbara Turner failing to find rare plants, including the endangered cream vetchling. At the time, she told me, with embarrassment, that she could indeed show me the vetchling and some of the other species, but she'd have to take me to a part of the preserve she had been avoiding—where she'd been violating Nature Preserves rules by mowing a small area for school-class gatherings. It turned out that "Leave it alone!" meant increasing shade, as trees and shrubs grew denser. Most of the woods had gotten too dark for many of its original species. The edge of the area Turner had kept open held the last of some species and was also the only place to find the oaks reproducing.

It began to be clear that nature needed more help than we thought. Under modern conditions, a few invasive species proliferate like cancer and replace the diverse natural ones. Water pollution, altered hydrology, and air quality changes all may require mitigations. Most Illinois ecosystems need fire. In many preserves, the high-quality acres of grassland, woodland, or wetland are surrounded with "buffer" land, which may protect the core from salt spray, herbicide drift, or the shade of tall buildings. But the buffers may harbor unnatural densities of invasives, predators, and parasites that thrive near edges. On the positive side, they may offer opportunities to expand the core. That can be crucial in the long run for some species, because many plant and especially animal species will not survive over time in small populations. Larger habitats and populations are more sustainable. Thus arose in nature preservation the unexpected need for restoration.

Aldo Leopold had done a bit of restoration himself. By today's standards, his efforts were primitive; but he thought deeply about the matter. He wrote:

Acts of creation are ordinarily reserved for gods and poets, but humbler folk may circumvent this restriction if they know how. To plant a pine, for example, one need be neither god nor poet; one need only own a shovel.

We have found restoration to require a good deal more than a shovel. Indeed, theoretical and practical education along with restraint and ethics are crucial.

By 1980, the Illinois Nature Preserves System consisted of seventy-nine preserves, including thirteen tallgrass prairies. But in that year, the System and George Fell were dealt a massive blow. With all their dedication and urgency, they had thought they possessed more power than they did. Suddenly, as George Fell perceived it, bureaucrats, politicians, and assembled forces opposed to preserve restrictions all conspired to get the Nature Preserves Commission's budget zeroed out by the Illinois legislature. The entire system seemed to be in danger.

It's a long story, but one result was that The Nature Conservancy hired me, and I finally got a "yes" to a proposal I'd been making for some time. While staff capacity was slowly being rebuilt, the Commission and the Conservancy would jointly sponsor a new group, the Volunteer Stewardship Network, to provide emergency care. Within a year, sixty preserves had volunteer

groups. Before long, hundreds of preserves were benefitting from thousands of stewards comprising another global first—a statewide community that May T. Watts would have commended.

Over time, as Nature Preserves staff was being rebuilt, these stewards were mentored by the best experts. They read books, attended classes, wrote newsletters, gave interviews to reporters, and organized conferences—building a "culture of conservation." They mended fences, cut brush, pulled weeds, helped with or led burns, installed signage—whatever was most needed.

Speaking of mending fences, during the 1990s some restoration opponents, believe it or not, got media coverage by criticizing the very concept of ecosystem management on the basis of both science and ethics, saying that "Leave nature alone!" was a better policy. Realizing that a consensus of expertise was needed, we took time to organize the Chicago Region Biodiversity Council (known popularly as "Chicago Wilderness"). With leadership by government, university, and not-for-profit conservationists, an authoritative Biodiversity Recovery Plan was assembled and approved in 1999. Some critics continued to complain, but now they were opposing one of the most impressive assemblages of conservation expertise on the planet, and they lost credibility.

Skills and interests vary enormously among agency staff and stewardship volunteers, and demands are such that a diverse human community is needed. Among the core constituency of volunteers, some show up on winter weekends to cut acres of brush. They burn it in bonfires, but keep warm mostly through muscle work and fellowship. Big machines could do much the same, but caring people do it with less stress on the ecosystem. And this attractive work is an entrance to the community.

Other people turn out every fall to harvest rare seeds. On "learn and lead" outings, new people regularly invoke hunter-gatherer images and values. Some develop an unexpected relationship. The biota seems to call out to us, that we are needed. It's a feeling that E. O. Wilson named "biophilia," a sense of affection for the diversity of life. Henry David Thoreau had written of this in his diary on October 10, 1858: "The simplest and most lumpish fungus has a peculiar interest to us… [it] betrays a life akin to my own. It is a successful poem in its kind."

In this massive effort, multiple roles and expertise are key. Some people learn to distinguish obscure species, monitor them, and inform the team of positive or concerning changes we might otherwise miss. Some become expert at recruiting, chain sawing, safe herbicide application, or controlled burn leadership. Some are adept at fostering collaborations between the volunteers and agency staff, essential to a thriving "conservation ecosystem."

Some of the roles are more unusual. We never expected plant sex to become a thing. But it turned out that on many sites the Federal Endangered prairie white-fringed orchid was failing to produce seed because of lack of co-adapted and highly specialized pollinators. How could we restore enough orchids to attract and rebuild hawk moth populations? Illinois Department of Natural Resources biologist Marlin Bowles taught us hand pollination. This process is so intimate, intricate, and sticky that some people find it embarrassing, at first. But scores do it, and moth and orchid numbers are on the rebound.

In my neighborhood in Northbrook, Illinois, we began learning to be stewards in 1977. Now, patches of restored Cook County Forest Preserve prairie, savanna, wetland, and woodland sprawl over 700 acres, attracting staff attention and a growing volunteer community. For five years as student, volunteer, and leader, Eriko Kojima has recruited, inspired, and taught one of the planet's most ambitious seed-gathering communities. In 2020, some 130 volunteers—despite having to work within the limits of COVID-19 social distancing—harvested local genotype seeds of 330 mostly uncommon or rare species, adding up to 490 gallons of seed mixes. The result is annually increasing quality for hundreds of acres.

When monitors noticed a failure-to-thrive in the peripheries between open savanna and open woodland, Sai Ramakrishna—for seven years a student, volunteer, and leader—took up the challenge and devised alternate seed mixes and strategies to test. This work is physically and intellectually demanding—and rewarding.

Ancient Culture Takes a Modern Form

The magic of fire has been appreciated by *Homo sapiens* since our beginnings. Today, among tallgrass biodiversity conservationists, fires that consume invasives and revive landscapes are now part of our seasonal lives, as are the harvest and broadcast of wild seeds. Stewards observe entire ecosystems rising or falling based on what we can accomplish, and we are inspired. Many experience this self-motivating dedication—and then stick with it for life. Culture needs long-term commitment.

Barbara Turner remained an active and passionate steward until her death at age 100 in 2020. She had learned from May Watts in the 1950s, who had learned from Henry Chandler Cowles, who wrote his first influential book in 1899. What Barbara left us in the Reed-Turner Woodland Nature Preserve now depends on us.

Such an ethic for the planet is urgently needed by the Earth's people. Some predict coming apocalyptic hellscapes and act as if they were inevitable. But is that the best we can do? Biodiversity conservationists act with hope, creativity, and grit. Our results motivate us to do more. Planetary health deserves celebration and growing commitment everywhere.

Today the Illinois Nature Preserves System includes 596 sites, totaling 115,061 acres. But constituency and funding have not kept pace. In 2015, some preserves were degrading from neglect, and a new five-year strategic plan warned that the system faced "dire economic, political, and landscape issues." As of 2019, the Nature Preserves System had received few of the recommended resources and had lacked a director and other senior staff for four years. Volunteer stewards took the initiative and, with the support of many professionals, launched Friends of Illinois Nature Preserves. The new not-for-profit group began organizing on-the-ground stewardship, constituency-building, and policy initiatives. In October 2020, a new governor's administration finally approved the hiring of the long-needed Nature Preserves director and agreed to provide more support. This is promising. But there will be ups and downs. The story of biodiversity conservation for the tallgrass region is still in its early stages.

I have purposely presented the land ethic as a product of social evolution because nothing so important as an ethic is ever 'written'... It evolved in the minds of a thinking community.

> –Aldo Leopold, "The Land Ethic"
> *A Sand County Almanac*

Leopold meant, of course, minds, bodies, and actions. Thoreau. Cowles. Watts. Leopold. Turner. Ramakrishna. Kojima. And so many people, now and throughout generations ahead, will determine our Earth's and biodiversity's future.

Following Robert Betz with his teaching and Torkel Korling with his photographs, Philip Juras has offered the world compelling art in this book. But the work was not finished when the paint dried. Dear reader and viewer, that work is ours as well. What generations accomplish depends not only on the film director, composer, parent, teacher, artist, land protector, or musician; it depends too on the actions of the people who receive their gifts. It depends upon all of us. When we succeed, a sustainable world of greater harmony and true richness will be our legacy.

A Vision of Restoration

by Philip Juras

Grigsby Prairie Flora, painting in progress, July 11, 2017.

One July morning as I began setting up my easel to paint at Grigsby Prairie in Barrington, Illinois, I was distracted by the remarkably loud and constant buzz of pollinators. Every size and shape of bee imaginable was arriving and departing from the blossoms of leadplant, coneflowers, and especially the prairie clover that surrounded me. But upon completing my painting a few hours later, all had gone silent. Later that day I would get a more complete understanding of the scene I had just experienced, a perfect demonstration in miniature of why tallgrass prairie restoration is so important.

I was first introduced to Grigsby Prairie five years before when nature educator Wendy Paulson suggested I visit the prairie restorations northwest of Chicago, some of them small remnants of the original prairie, and some reestablished on former farm fields. Wendy knew I was passionate about grasslands, being familiar with my southeastern work. On that first trip in 2013, I was smitten. The glorious July flora of Galloping Hill Prairie and

Poplar Creek Prairie, both jewels of the Forest Preserves of Cook County, enthralled me. So did Flint Creek Savanna, the home base for Citizens for Conservation, a volunteer group with near-magical powers to bring prairie ecosystems back to life. In these preserves, I was witnessing what might be called the Chicago style of restoration, where community and government organizations, propelled by motivated knowledgeable citizens, have turned parcel after parcel into gorgeous, functioning nature preserves. The more I saw, the more my own understanding of the possibilities and benefits of conservation grew.

Grigsby Prairie, another Citizens for Conservation preserve, was an example of this. There, on a summer morning in 2013, I first met the late Tom Vanderpoel, the generous-hearted mastermind behind so many of CFC's restorations. Walking the narrow winding path through Grigsby's seamlessly-merging habitats, Tom pointed out the magic behind the curtain—the decades of trial and error and nuanced approach to everything from weed control and wetland construction, to the artful matching of cohorts of species with the various soils and moisture levels of the 42-acre site. The effect on this former farm field was as if Mother Nature herself had re-created a prairie in suburban Chicago.

The day I painted the July flora of Grigsby Prairie with its attendant bees, I visited Tom and his wife Gail, who shares his passion for restoration. After I relayed my observation of the vanishing pollinators, Tom got out one of the biggest books I've ever seen, *Flora of the Chicago Region* by Gerould Wilhelm and Laura Rericha. Looking up "purple prairie clover," we learned that an astounding sixty-four kinds of bees collect its pollen and nectar, the pollen usually being exhausted by 10 a.m. To have just witnessed that interaction, where the prairie (and prairie clovers) had been absent for a century, seemed miraculous.

Chicago area restorations that Wendy and Tom introduced me to, such as Grigsby, Poplar Creek, and Galloping Hill, and the people who make them possible, became a springboard to wider exploration of Illinois' tallgrass ecosystem. However, this wasn't my first experience of the Prairie State.

My mother was born and lived in Illinois before moving away for college. The stories I heard growing up in Georgia, in which "prairie" meant a vast agricultural landscape, reinforced by the few times I had visited Illinois as a child, gave me further cause to want to explore it. What's more, I discovered on my first drive to Chicago from my home in Athens, Georgia, that many of the state's far-flung preserves could be included in my itinerary—and there are some real gems among them. This was, at long last, a chance for me to explore and paint a subject that's fascinated me for years.

As an artist, it feels quite natural to be enthralled by tallgrass prairie. Its sublime aesthetics, rich ecology, and fascinating history are the essential ingredients for what I believe creates a compelling landscape painting. I became acquainted with these aspects while studying landscape architecture under Professor Darrel Morrison, an Iowan who taught designing with nature at the University of Georgia. There, I researched pre-European southeastern grasslands and found a subject that would drive much of my work in subsequent years. I have since painted many variations of grasslands in the Southeast, which have much in common with the midwestern tallgrass prairie. In fact, I think of the Southeast as something of a home base for the tallgrass prairie ecosystem. As I learned in *Forgotten Grasslands of the South* by Reed Noss, the region's ancient grasslands provided a refuge for tallgrass prairie species during glaciation. Today, they actually harbor a greater variety of plants with grassland affinities than are found in the prairie region. In Illinois, the small rocky glades and hill prairies on its southern end link those unglaciated refugia with the wide variety of post-glacial prairie landscapes that once covered most of the state. Between them is a treasure trove of botanical and scenic diversity, hidden

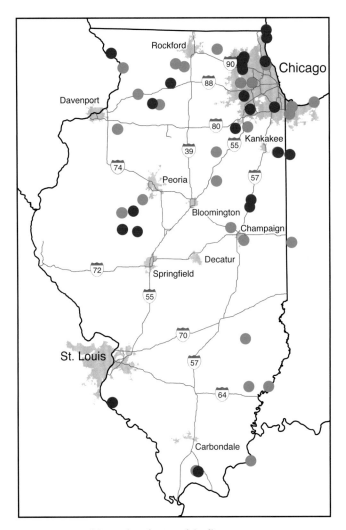

Preserves visited (green) and painted (red).

like jewels among vast expanses of cropland, each with inviting aesthetics and background stories to inspire further exploration.

Considering its origins, disappearance, and restoration, tallgrass prairie became an irresistible subject to me. How did these archetypal grasslands exist east of the Mississippi River, where there is generally enough annual moisture to support forest growth? What did they look like, how did they come to be, and what would it be like to stand in the middle of one? Questions like these inspire me. Place me in any landscape in the United States and I'll immediately start wondering what it used to be like before European settlement—and if any evidence of it still exists. That's a challenge in Illinois. With only .01% of its original tallgrass prairie remaining, it's hard to imagine the pre-Columbian prairie, especially at a landscape scale. I did get some sense of its immensity while driving through long stretches of featureless corn and soybean fields, but it was in visiting its preserves, managed by state and nonprofit organizations, that I was able to observe some historic prairie characteristics firsthand.

On one such memorable occasion, Randy Nyboer of the Illinois Natural History Survey introduced me to Foley Sand Prairie, a 15-acre nature preserve that straddles a low sand dune in Lee County. He explained that the tiny remnant before us had never been plowed, and that we were in fact standing upon an original piece of the great American prairie—and I was moved. The sensation was reinforced by the colorful diversity of prairie plants at our feet and the open landscape around us. With a little imagination and careful framing of the scenery it was almost possible to envision that prairie rolling all the way to the horizon. To fully realize that impression, at Foley and at all of the remnants and restorations I've visited, I looked to historic accounts and literature. Artist George Catlin's description of his 1834 solo journey across the prairies of Missouri and Willa Cather's *My Ántonia* were two favorites for revealing the first-person experience of the original tallgrass landscape. For Illinois, *Of Prairie, Woods, and Water*, edited by Joel Greenberg, and Robert Betz's *The Prairie of the Illinois Country* gave me the clearest picture of the sites I was visiting.

I also looked to American landscape painting from the time of westward expansion. I had hoped to find detailed depictions of the vast unbroken prairies that still existed in the nineteenth century to help me imagine the original Illinois prairie in its fullness; but as art historian Joni L. Kinsey lays out in *Plain Pictures, Images of the American Prairie*, artists at that time were deterred from depicting the prairie because it lacked the traditional compositional elements they

Alvan Fisher (1792–1863), *The Prairie on Fire,* 1827, Oil on canvas, 24 x 33 in., The Art Institute of Chicago.
Fisher depicts a scene from James Fenimore Cooper's *The Prairie* in which Natty Bumppo creates a fire break to save his companions.

Junius R. Sloan (1827-1900), *Cool Morning on the Prairie,* 1866, Oil on canvas on Masonite, 17 1/4 x 34 3/16 in., Gift of Percy H. Sloan, Brauer Museum of Art, 53.01.070, Valparaiso University.
Sloan, whose family farm was in Kewanee, Illinois, relies on the diminishing size of cows and fencing to convey depth of space in this prairie scene.

relied on, such as trees and rocks to frame the view and an elevated vantage point. They would have found little to frame the wide horizons of large swaths of presettlement Illinois. They could, however, use imported features such as a horse and rider or a prairie fire to give structure and context. With the prairie as a backdrop, such views were mainly concerned with a human vs. nature narrative, revealing how challenging and powerful the original prairie was, but not providing much descriptive information about the prairie itself. Eventually settlement brought enough structure to the prairie to satisfy the compositional needs of nineteenth century artists, but it wasn't until the twentieth century, after art movements like abstraction and minimalism, that the empty nature of the prairie would again appeal. Unfortunately, by then the original prairie was gone.

As a traditionally-inclined landscape painter, I also discovered the challenges of the prairie environment. Even in the small preserves I visited, the horizon was pervasive, and the foreground was often sparse. Vertical enclosing features I'm so familiar with in my home environment— such as foreground trees framing the view—might be found on the edges, but were often incompatible with what the preserve represented, and thus with my painting. That was even more true when picturing the landscape of the Grand Prairie on drives across the state, the

Philip Juras, *Sunset*, Little St. Simons Island, Georgia, 2013, Oil on canvas, 12 x 16 in.

overwhelming horizontality of its cornfields restrained only by the window frames of my car. My closest comparable experience of landscape comes from the salt marshes of the southeastern Atlantic coast, which present similar challenges in their flat expanses of marsh grass. In either case, the sky attains utmost importance, while island-like clumps of trees become focal points, and foreground features like watercourses or animal trails offer the viewer an inviting pathway into the scene. On the other hand, a minimally embellished view with an unbroken horizon can also provide a contemplative narrative, even if less compositionally accommodating.

In any case, I invite the viewer to stand in the grasses with me and view the scenes in this book as a window into the aesthetic of tallgrass prairie environments. To make the experience as tangible as possible, I have been faithful in differentiating plant species and rendering topography and atmospheric effects, but hopefully doing so in a painterly enough way to be true to an overall impression or feeling of the place.

In framing my compositions, I have largely avoided showing signs of modernity, so that with the exception of the presettlement views, the viewer can place the scene in the present, past, or future. But that is not to say that human impact is not present in all of these images. In spite of my initial motivation to rediscover an ecosystem unaltered by modern humans, I have found cultural influence fundamental to each and every scene I've painted. Obviously, that's true where prairies now occupy former cornfields, but even in the best tallgrass prairie remnants, where I had imagined the patterns, textures, and forms would reveal the timeless natural processes that built them, I found the human story to be of equal or greater importance.

Of course, none of the remnants I've visited would still exist without recent stewardship efforts that keep invasive plants and encroaching trees from suffocating them, or development or agriculture from obliterating them. And

Philip Juras, *Oak Island*, Nachusa Grasslands, Illinois, June 12, 2018, Oil on canvas, 8 x 16 in.

there were the less intentional actions of past generations, including postsettlement activities of grazing, burning, and burying, that allowed patches to persist in backlots, along railroad tracks, and in pioneer cemeteries. But perhaps the most fundamental human contribution in promoting tall-grass prairie happened before the arrival of Europeans. For thousands of years, Native Americans burned the prairies to manage the landscape to their advantage. Their fires, added to those caused by lightning, are likely what tipped the scale against forests. Otherwise, European settlers might have been clearing trees rather than turning sod when they usurped Indigenous lands. As it was then, fire remains essential for maintaining prairie environments today.

A highlight of my Illinois adventures was participating as both painter and fully trained wildland firefighter and "fire lighter" on several prescribed fires at The Nature Conservancy's Nachusa Grasslands, a 3,800-acre preserve near Franklin Grove, Illinois. Under the adept direction of

Nachusa's manager Bill Kleiman, our crew burned several patches of restored prairie, echoing the practices of the Native Americans; in essence, we were contributing to the perpetuation of a cultural landscape. Yet, when painting in those same patches, engrossed by the flowering forbs and roaming bison of summer, I would forget the human involvement—the burning, weeding, planting, and managing—and simply revel in the nature before me.

On the afternoon of June 12, 2018, I found myself in such a revery when I was interrupted from my painting by Nachusa's bison. The herd, which was featured in my composition, started wandering my way. Sitting safely in the open cab of the utility vehicle I was using, I was enveloped in a soundscape of snuffling and soft tearing and munching of mouthfuls of prairie grass as the group shuffled past. Around us, birds sang, pollinators buzzed, and a breeze ruffled the grasses. With a thousand acres of Nachusa's blooming prairies and savannas around me, I couldn't help but feel that the sensory impressions I was experiencing would have been much the same on the wild, pre-Columbian tallgrass prairie. Yet it was an entirely modern experience, an effect achieved through the powerful combination of dedicated volunteers and organizational expertise that had converted cow pastures and cornfields back to functioning tallgrass prairie—replete with native megafauna. Now even the bison are chipping in, creating habitat for the return of the upland sandpiper and other native species through their grazing, trampling, and wallowing.

My preoccupation with presettlement nature causes me a certain amount of cognitive dissonance when taking in the seemingly timeless beauty of a human-altered place like Nachusa Grasslands, Grigsby Prairie, or even Foley Sand Prairie. Like most Americans of my time, I was raised on the founding myths of the uncivilized wilderness offered by Providence to accommodate American progress. We know now that it's a far more complicated and often horrific story. The tallgrass prairie and other fire-managed presettlement cultural environments illuminate that history in a more accurate light. To set foot in a prairie or savanna, or to paint one, is a way to make a genuine personal connection with the generations that preceded us. It's also an opportunity to connect with those who carry the torch for prairie conservation today.

From the Wisconsin border to the bluffs of the Ohio River, I'm grateful to have had that opportunity. Granted, a dozen trips over six years didn't allow enough time to see all I wanted to see in such a large area, but I reached a wide range of environments, from mesic black-soil prairies and morainal wetlands to xeric oak savannas and parched limestone bluffs. Although my sample of sites was limited, observations of topography, species composition, seasonal aspects, atmospheric effects, and tree enclosure provided the material for the picture I hoped to create—a comprehensive view of the tallgrass prairie ecosystem in form, pattern, texture, and color.

This book, and my corresponding exhibition at the Chicago Botanic Garden, assembles the most compelling scenes from my explorations—moments where I was awed by the natural beauty before me, and inspired by the human history of these places. The paintings, all oil on canvas, are arranged on the following pages to generally reflect the tallgrass prairie themes that have most captivated me: flora, land meeting sky, woodlands, seasons, agents of biodiversity, wetlands, and presettlement history. Each image is accompanied by text describing key ecological, historical, and aesthetic aspects, as well as something of my experience of the place.

Throughout this project I've been guided by several remarkable prairie experts, among them Stephen Packard, who has not only enriched the tallgrass region with his work—and now this book with his words—but has also had a hand in shaping most of the landscapes I've painted. I am grateful to Stephen, his fellow conservationists, and all those who came before to bring this important grassland ecosystem back to life, not only making it possible for me to picture the prairie, but also ensuring that all of us can reconnect with this uniquely beautiful ecosystem. These paintings celebrate their achievements, while inviting all who enjoy nature's beauty to join in, to hike a trail in a nearby preserve where the state, county, or a nonprofit has restored the prairie. I think visitors to these places will find, as I have, that the glorious diversity of plants and animals that make up one of the most storied ecosystems in North America is worthy of our reverence and care.

The Paintings

Picturing the Prairie

Like painting, tallgrass prairie restoration is an act of creation, but when all goes well it yields far more than aesthetic beauty. Galloping Hill Prairie, a former pasture in Cook County's Spring Creek (also called Spring Lake) Forest Preserve, embodies that. It was one of the first restorations I visited in July 2013 as I began my exploration of Illinois prairies. My previous notions of what a restoration could be were surpassed by its colorful blooms rising to meet the sky on a verdant wave. And what a sky—animated cumulus and cirrus clouds seeming to echo the prairie's name. In the years since, visiting prairie restorations and remnants across the state, I have happily encountered these aspects again and again, to the point that Galloping Hill seems like an early celebration of them all.

In this view, gray-headed coneflowers and wild bergamot provide the greatest color contrast to the green of the prairie, particularly toward the crest of the morainal rise. Rattlesnake master, compass plant, rosinweed, mountain mint, and big bluestem are all distinguishable among the various forbs and grasses, but I took the liberty of leaving out Queen Anne's lace and other weedy non-natives. They will largely disappear over time anyway, as dedicated volunteers work with the county to nurture this splendid restoration.

Galloping Hill Prairie, Cook County, Illinois, 2019, Oil on canvas, 36 x 48 in.

In a 1989 article in the *Chicago Tribune*, Stephen Packard, then head of The Nature Conservancy in Illinois stewardship program, said of the initial effort to restore Poplar Creek Prairie, "In twenty to thirty years, it will still be an immature prairie. But by then we'll be seeing what it can become, and the abundance of wildlife that it can nourish and draw."

It was a sky-blue July morning twenty-four years later when Wendy Paulson first led me along a narrow footpath through the waist-high foliage of that very same mesic prairie. It was the largest tallgrass prairie restoration I had yet seen, and I was enthralled by the expansive drifts of flowering forbs and luxurious grasses. It was hard to imagine it had ever been a cornfield. As we progressed, soaked to the waist with morning dew, Wendy pointed out a Henslow's sparrow perched on a compass plant, asserting its territory for the nesting season. As a threatened tallgrass prairie species, its presence was a testament to Stephen's vision of decades earlier.

In this studio painting inspired by our July visit, a seasonal tide of big bluestem, tall coreopsis, and the yellow flowers of compass plants have begun to obscure the view of the horizon. Below them, lavender-flowering wild bergamot and bright yellow gray-headed coneflowers, which are often abundant in restored prairies, compete for space with the off-white blooms of wild quinine and the not-yet-flowering stems of stiff goldenrod. These are only a handful of over 100 species of prairie plants that have been lovingly restored to this former farm site by the Poplar Creek Prairie Stewards, a volunteer group working with the Forest Preserves of Cook County, with initial support from The Nature Conservancy. For thirty years they have worked to restore hundreds of acres of tallgrass prairie and oak savanna at Poplar Creek, part of the Arthur L. Janura Forest Preserve in Hoffman Estates.

Inspired by Poplar Creek Prairie, Cook County, Illinois, 2013, Oil on canvas, 24 x 36 in.

Grigsby Prairie Flora, Lake County, Illinois, July 11, 2017, Oil on canvas, 14 x 18 in.

Grigsby Prairie's range of environments, from wet prairie potholes to dry/mesic uplands, made it tough to choose the right composition to highlight the biodiversity of this restoration in Barrington. Citizens for Conservation, the volunteer organization that owns Grigsby, has restored 175 native prairie species to these 42.2 acres of former farmland over the last thirty years. With aesthetic abundance at every turn, I eventually decided on a drier upland setting for my composition. Like the plentiful pollinators I encountered there, I was attracted to a show of purple and white prairie clovers complemented by the blooms of pale purple coneflower, lead plant, coreopsis, and black-eyed Susans.

Those floral details, and the coarse-shaped leaves of forbs such as compass plant, were nicely set off by a grassy background of fine-textured prairie dropseed.

Genshurg Markham Prairie, Cook County, Illinois, July 10, 2017, Oil on canvas, 9 x 11 in.

It is a moving experience to set foot in a true prairie remnant, ponder the profusion of flowers and grasses, and imagine how the patch of prairie in front of you could have once extended across millions of acres of Illinois and beyond. The rich virgin prairies that were the foundation of Illinois' extraordinary agricultural wealth are now functionally extinct as an ecosystem, existing today only in tiny unplowed fragments. Without the protection and management of motivated individuals and nonprofit and governmental organizations, even those fragments would be gone.

To appreciate what remains and to better understand the historic tallgrass ecosystem, I visited several preserves with mesic, wet mesic, and black-soil components. I painted a few of them as well. My studies from the Gensburg Markham (left), Prospect Cemetery (p. 38), and Loda Cemetery (p. 39) prairies record my impressions of some of their predominant aesthetic characteristics. I used these later to inform a larger, imagined view of the presettlement prairie (p. 96). All three of these prairie remnants are part of the Illinois Nature Preserves System, protecting rare plants, animals, and other unique natural features across the state. Sixteen such preserves are featured in this book.

Painted quickly between summer rain showers, my study of Gensburg Markham Prairie explores the wide range of patterns, textures, and colors produced by the rich species diversity in a mesic section of this extraordinary prairie remnant. Species depicted include prairie dock, purple prairie clover, smooth phlox, Culver's root, prairie coreopsis, wild bergamot, and prairie dropseed. A National Natural Landmark, the 167-acre preserve sits in the former lake plain of Glacial Lake Chicago and its sandy and clayey soils support a mosaic of prairie communities. It is managed by Northeastern Illinois University and The Nature Conservancy.

Prospect Cemetery Prairie, Ford County, Illinois, August 17, 2019, Oil on canvas, 9 x 12 in.

L azy summer afternoon doldrums were no match for the excitement of exploring and then capturing an impression of the real McCoy—a small piece of the original Grand Prairie of Illinois. Established in 1859 and never plowed, this segment of Prospect Cemetery, just a few acres in size, had all the colorful diversity I would have imagined in a high-quality black-soil prairie remnant.

Prominent in the view I selected were prairie dock, blazing star, rattlesnake master, big bluestem, and the dormant heads of coneflowers—and there was so much more in every direction. I might not have had any subjects to choose from had the state not dedicated this cemetery as a preserve in 1976.

Loda Cemetery Prairie, Iroquois County, Illinois, August 17, 2019, Oil on canvas, 9 x 12 in.

With 130 native plant species in a little over three acres, Loda Cemetery Prairie is one of the best black-soil remnants in the state. It was preserved in 1981 when the Natural Land Institute, The Nature Conservancy in Illinois, and Grand Prairie Friends helped the adjacent Pine Ridge Cemetery meet its expansion needs by swapping this reserved patch of unplowed burial ground for adjacent cornfields. Since then, the Friends, now full owners, have purchased and are restoring a further nine acres to buffer the remnant. Before I started my painting there, I encountered a colorful cicada making its loud rasping call. Prairie cicadas are only found in unplowed remnants and are as rare as the sight of an original prairie sweeping toward the western horizon.

Chiwaukee Prairie, Kenosha County, Wisconsin, 2019, Oil on canvas, 36 x 48 in.

Sand Prairie, Illinois Beach State Park, Illinois, July 26, 2015, Oil on canvas, 10 x 16 in.

Over 400 plant species can be found in the remnant dune and swale environment of Chiwaukee Prairie, a Wisconsin State Natural Area on the shore of Lake Michigan. This National Natural Landmark is part of the Chiwaukee Prairie-Illinois Beach Lake Plain, an area of globally important wetlands and prairies north of Waukegan, Illinois. It's popular with birders, botanists, and picnickers, and I too was drawn to the area. I was first inspired by the remnant sand prairies and oak savannas of Illinois Beach State Park, where I painted a small study. Later that day I was dazzled by the display at Chiwaukee Prairie.

My studio painting of Chiwaukee records the day's final moments, when the dull overcast suddenly gave way to a sky worthy of the prairie's spectacular remnant flora. In the dimming light, rosinweed, black-eyed Susan, blazing star, wild onion, common mountain mint, St. John's wort, spirea, and spiderwort animated the foreground of the scene, while further back, bands of colors and forms in the vegetation revealed the wet swales and low, dry sand ridges that are the foundation of the prairie's high diversity.

As a prime location between Chicago and Milwaukee, Chiwaukee was threatened by growth more than once. A 1920s development was halted by the Great Depression, but it was local citizens, working with The Nature Conservancy, who protected this site—the last of its kind in the world—from development in the 1960s.

From small, overgrazed remnants, first noticed by prairie enthusiasts Doug and Dot Wade in the 1970s, The Nature Conservancy and Friends of Nachusa Grasslands have restored functioning prairie to thousands of acres of former agricultural fields and overgrown woodlands near Franklin Grove. In those acres I've explored a wide range of prairie aspects, from flora and fauna to prescribed fire and seasonal change, but perhaps I've been most captivated by the combination of open prairie and wide-open skies.

In this July view from Doug's Knob (named for Doug Wade), with Nachusa's prairie stretching to the horizon, all that open space is a perfect stage set for the gilding of both sky and landscape as the low sun lights up the moisture-laden atmosphere. The foreground has a warm tone too, but with subtle distinctions.

Had this section of Nachusa been burned in the previous fire season, the color cast of backlit stems would be exclusively yellow to green. As it is, the dew-laden dead stems from last year pick up both the cool color of the sky and the orange of the sunrise.

Sunrise, Nachusa Grasslands, Illinois, 2019, Oil on canvas, 36 x 54 in.

In this October view, the sun now sets directly behind Doug's Knob, the location of the viewpoint of the previous painting (p. 43). As a counterpoint to the moist atmosphere in that morning view, the air is now crisp, drawing a sharp contrast along the horizon line of grass, trees, and sky.

Thirty years ago, and for many decades prior, the bottomlands in this scene were covered with corn and soybeans fenced off from the cows that grazed the small hills too rocky to plow. It was on those hills that the prairie species persisted, supplying the seed bank for the restoration of the surrounding fields. The handful of trees on the nearest knoll mark the edges of one of those former fence lines.

In 2013, nearly a third of Nachusa, including this core area, was dedicated as an Illinois Nature Preserve.

Sunset, Nachusa Grasslands, Illinois, 2019, Oil on canvas, 36 x 54 in.

Foley Sand Prairie, an Illinois Nature Preserve at the western edge of Lee County, though small, connects prairie with sky as rising topography and wide-open farmland obscure the distant treeline. Perhaps because of that, I felt I stood in the historic great American prairie when I first set foot there. The main attraction of this forty-year-old state preserve is the never-plowed 15-acre dry prairie that occupies the low dune spanning the site. Viewed from its base as in this autumn scene, an ecological and aesthetic shift can be observed in its visually dominant grasses. Moisture-loving prairie cordgrass, with its long arcing leaves in the lower right foreground, gives way to big bluestem a little higher on the slope as the soil moisture decreases. In turn, the big bluestem's warm-colored vertical stalks rise toward the horizon line and blend into the reddish tint of little bluestem, the prominent grass occupying the dry ridge top. It's a shift from wet to dry, from coarse to fine, and from green to red, all beneath a blue and white September sky.

The moisture gradient is also apparent in my June field study of Foley (left). Here, the blue green of prairie cordgrass marks the wetter base of the dune with a virtual cloud of pale purple coneflower capping the dry dune ridge. Flecks and bands of color suggest the plethora of other species in bloom, including common milkweed, white false indigo, prairie lily, prairie coreopsis, and wild quinine. By September these will be going dormant, showing mainly their yellowing leaves and dry seed heads, as will many of the 160 native species of the preserve.

Color Study, Foley Sand Prairie, Lee County, Illinois, June 14, 2018, Oil on canvas, 8 x 11 in.

Foley Sand Prairie, Lee County, Illinois, 2019, Oil on canvas, 36 x 60 in.

Winter Evening, Sand Prairie-Scrub Oak Nature Preserve, Mason County, Illinois, 2019, Oil on canvas, 36 x 60 in.

An hour south of Peoria, the state's Sand Prairie-Scrub Oak Nature Preserve offers an example of an historic prairie ecosystem that developed in the post-glacial era on wind-deposited sand east (downwind) of major river drainages. Thousands of acres of these sand prairies still existed in Illinois before the mid-twentieth century, after which the invention of center-pivot irrigation made them profitable for agricultural use.

Little bluestem, the visually dominant grass in this scene, shares space in the sand prairie with goat's rue, eastern prickly pear cactus, sand love grass, and porcupine grass. Blackjack oak, one of which is the focal point of this painting, is co-dominant in the surrounding sand savanna and dry sand forests with black oak, mockernut hickory, and black hickory. The scattering of fire-intolerant eastern redcedars and the size and density of the oaks in the surrounding groves suggest this prairie receives a lot less fire than it would have before European settlement.

With daylight fading, I had abandoned my explorations of these grassy openings, but as I began to drive away, this scene appeared in my passenger's side window, prompting a few more quiet moments among the warm-colored grasses and icy patches of December.

Perched on a limestone cliff high above Kidd Lake and the Mississippi River floodplain, Fults Hill Prairie Nature Preserve is perhaps the most exotic of the prairie remnants I have visited in Illinois. On my May 2019 visit I found a view from a convenient deer trail that captured several of its springtime features. Standing on that trail, clinging to the steep loess slope, I could almost reach out horizontally to touch the blooms of hoary puccoon, pale beardtongue, small skullcap, and the new leaves of many other forbs rising from the recently burned prairie. Below me, fire-pruned eastern redcedars along the cliff edge hinted at the regularity of the prescribed fires that keep this phenomenal prairie from being shaded out by encroaching trees. The whole experience was enlivened by the constant chatter of migratory birds rising from the flooded wetlands and forests below, while a moisture-laden sky, almost low enough to meet the vertical green slopes, further enhanced the scene.

Fults Hill Prairie, Monroe County, Illinois, 2019, Oil on canvas, 30 x 48 in.

Tawny Slopes, Revis Hill Prairie Nature Preserve, Mason County, Illinois, May 9, 2019, Oil on canvas, 9 x 12 in.

Like sand prairies, loess hill prairies and sand hill prairies developed on post-glacial wind deposits. The fine silt particles and chemical makeup of loess allow its eroded landforms to become rather steep. Indeed, I was surprised to find some slopes at Revis Hill Prairie, an Illinois Nature Preserve, too steep to climb. In this spring view, with daylight fading, I was struck both by the pronounced terrain and the tawny clumps of last year's grasses. Unlike Fults Hill Prairie which I had visited earlier that day, this section of Revis had not been burned in the prior season. After painting until dark, I descended the slopes accompanied by a night hawk swooping and calling along the wooded edge below.

Goat Prairie, Hanover Bluff State Natural Area, Illinois, September 30, 2016, Oil on canvas, 12.25 x 18 in.

After a steep climb through a lush forest, it was a delight to emerge into a flowery glade with inspiring views at Hanover Bluff. This sand hill prairie, or "goat prairie" (of little use to farmers except for grazing their goats), presented me with a magnificent western panorama of the Mississippi River valley and the bottomland sand prairies of the old Savanna Army Depot. But I was swayed by the view to the north, in which the tilted foreground of goldenrods, asters, and little bluestem led to the next hillside goat prairie, enticing me to explore further. Encircled by encroaching trees, these sun-loving prairie species–and the panoramic vistas–depend on burning and clearing by the state to keep them open, a common theme in hill prairies throughout the region.

Eastward-blown stalks of little bluestem in The Nature Conservancy's Pembroke Savanna indicate the predominant wind direction that formed these large sand dunes in the post-glacial era. I was inspired by a late afternoon visit in May 2019 to find a composition that would highlight that remarkable dune topography along with the savanna's characteristic black oaks, bird-foot violets, and plains pocket gopher excavations. These gophers reach the eastern end of their range at Pembroke, and like little bioengineers, their excavations diversify the savanna by creating patches of barren soil for seed germination. Their warm-colored mounds fit in nicely with the striking color combination of new spring growth, last year's golden grass stems, and a deep blue sky.

These savannas have persisted thanks in part to their sandy unproductive soils, and also the traditions and landscape practices of the rural African American community that has long called Pembroke Township home. A mutually beneficial relationship between the community and conservation organizations would be the savannas' best bet for the future. I imagine the local population of quail would agree, Pembroke being ideal habitat for this threatened grassland bird. I had heard their call at other preserves like Nachusa Grasslands, Beadles Barrens, and Fults Hill Prairie, so in the quiet beauty of Pembroke it was reassuring to hear "Bob-White" chime in with the chatter of spring migrants.

Pembroke Savanna, Kankakee County, Illinois, 2019, Oil on canvas, 30 x 48 in.

Cave Creek Glade Preserve, Johnson County, Illinois, 2020, Oil on canvas, 24 x 36 in.

Looking out across the Gulf Coastal Plain at the southern end of Illinois after climbing a steep boulder-strewn trail on a sultry, breezy May afternoon, it was almost hard to believe I was still in the Prairie State. Ascending the hill, I was greeted by prairie classics such as big bluestem and prairie dock, and higher up, little bluestem and pale purple coneflower. At the top, however, the steep limestone glade transitioned to a dry upland forest of stunted post and chinquapin oaks that beautifully framed the southwestern view. Understory species featured in this fire-managed scene include serviceberry and redbud trees, as well as herbaceous plants such as pale penstemon, wild bergamot, yellow pimpernel, and various other forbs and grasses.

Perhaps because this state nature preserve is outside of the zone of the Pleistocene glaciation, Cave Creek reminded me of grasslands further to the south. Southeastern grasslands, including glades like this one, were refugia for prairie species during glacial episodes.

Somme Prairie Grove, Cook County, Illinois, August 19, 2019, Oil on canvas, 8 x 12 in.

Even rarer than unplowed prairie, ecologically intact tallgrass savannas have virtually disappeared. Among their scattered oaks, diversity could exceed that of adjacent prairies and woodlands, as they drew species from both, while specializing in a few more of their own. Somme Prairie Grove, surrounded by metropolitan Chicago, is both a garden oasis and laboratory of savanna restoration. Volunteer efforts shepherded by Stephen Packard since the 1970s have transformed this badly tattered remnant into a treasure for human and natural communities alike. For the artist, the choices of subject there are many. One August morning, I selected the edge of a woodland grove for this field painting, where a bank of rosinweed, sweet black-eyed Susan, and showy tick trefoil set the stage for a cohort of young bur oaks.

Bur Oak, Flint Creek Savanna, Lake County, Illinois, July 11, 2017, Oil on canvas, 10 x 16 in.

Aldo Leopold wrote that "he who owns a veteran bur oak owns more than a tree. He owns a historical library, and a reserved seat in the theater of evolution."

The old bur oaks of Flint Creek Savanna speak volumes of this former farm site's tallgrass prairie past. Alone or in groves, their stately presence anchors the savanna, prairie, and wetland restorations that began there in 1988, when Citizens for Conservation first purchased the land. In my perambulations along the preserve's narrow paths, I was repeatedly awed by their majestic stature and expressive, characteristic form.

R estored largely by the Poplar Creek Prairie Stewards starting in 1989, this former farmer's woodlot retains many open-growth trees that characterize the region's original woodlands. It, and the adjacent Poplar Creek Prairie (p. 33), owe much of their current richness to the efforts of these dedicated volunteers. Visitors can now experience an open canopy and diverse understory not unlike what early settlers would have seen. In this September view of the grove, bur and white oaks cast late afternoon shade across the seed heads of sweet Joe-Pye weed, bottlebrush grass, and elm-leaved and other goldenrods, while Drummond's aster blooms in the foreground.

Recently renamed as the Carl R. Hansen Woods in honor of the former Cook County Commissioner who saved it from becoming a landfill, the woods are part of the Arthur L. Janura Forest Preserve, commonly known as the Poplar Creek Forest Preserve, in Hoffman Estates.

Shoe Factory Road Woods, Cook County, Illinois, 2020, Oil on canvas, 30 x 42 in.

The Woods, Nachusa Grasslands, Illinois, October 21, 2017, Oil on canvas, 18 x 26 in.

Looking west from the visitor center, an observer will notice that Nachusa's open prairie transitions to savannas and then woodlands as it nears Franklin Creek. The existence of these woodlands can be traced to the shielding effect that the creek, and the Rock River beyond, had in reducing the intensity of wildfires blowing in from the open plains further west. With settlement, those fires were extinguished, and trees invaded where land wasn't plowed or grazed. The Nature Conservancy and Friends of Nachusa Grasslands have used prescribed fire and selective clearing to reopen some of those overgrown woodlands, releasing their sun-loving herbaceous species and reestablishing the rich ecological transition from prairie to woodland. The resulting configuration of topography, trees, and openings makes a compelling painting subject, more so when tinged with fall colors. On the windy October day I spent painting in the woodlands, I took a fair amount of time to render the various branching patterns in the different kinds of trees. With the sky consistently blue, I had ample time to finish up, although I did have to tie my easel to a tree to keep it from blowing away.

It goes without saying that there is a seasonal aspect to any landscape painting of the tallgrass ecosystem, but to explore seasonal qualities more fully, it helps to do it in one place. Over the years I have been repeatedly drawn to a distinctive grove of oaks perched atop Doug's Knob, a high-quality hilltop prairie remnant at the heart of the Nachusa Grasslands. While my visits weren't frequent enough to capture all of the floral changes of the growing season, so celebrated in early descriptions of the unbroken prairie, these six paintings (pp. 65–75) do convey many of the changing colors and textures of tallgrass prairie through the year. Each was begun on location and some were completed there, giving them a looser, more immediate feel. Those completed in the studio tend to appear more finished.

May 11 was too late to see pasque flowers and a little early for shooting stars, but new green shoots emerging en masse from the formerly barren surface more than conveyed the feeling of the season. Wind, light rain, and sleet hampered my initial progress on this painting, but it was completely halted by the arrival of Nachusa's bison herd. The work was finished later in the undisturbed comfort of the indoors.

Doug's Knob, May, Nachusa Grasslands, Illinois, May 11, 2019, Oil on canvas, 18 x 26 in.

In June, a little higher on the hillside, the remnant population of pale purple coneflower, wild quinine, spiderwort, leadplant, prickly prairie rose, and other flowers bloom among a rising tide of porcupine grass, little bluestem, and prairie dropseed. The presence in the foreground of last year's dead grass stems reveal that this area wasn't burned in the previous fire season. With consistent light and weather, I had time to finish this on site.

Doug's Knob, June, Nachusa Grasslands, Illinois, June 13, 2018, Oil on canvas, 18 x 26 in.

In July, a bit lower on the slope, an abundance of gray-headed coneflower and wild bergamot, which are often very showy in prairie restorations, highlight the transition from the remnant prairie above to the formerly plowed base of the knob. The profusion of blooms in the foreground necessitated completing this, my first view of Doug's Knob, at a later date.

Doug's Knob, July, Nachusa Grasslands, Illinois, July 28, 2015, Oil on canvas, 18 x 26 in.

A robust growth of goldenrod, asters, and big bluestem on the lower slope set a warm, lively tone at the end of September. A woodchuck burrow, also evident in the May painting (p. 65), is still visible high on the slope, since the prairie never gets very tall in the dry gravelly soils on top of the knob. The conditions were breezy but otherwise ideal to finish this painting. Three years later I would choose the exact same spot for my May composition.

Doug's Knob, September, Nachusa Grasslands, Illinois, September 28, 2016, Oil on canvas, 18 x 26 in.

From the south side of Doug's Knob, little bluestem dominates the view. Its prevalence in this section is a result of having to control the broadleaf weeds that followed years of cattle grazing. It will take a bit longer here to establish the diversity found on other parts of the knob, but in the meantime, the texture and color of little bluestem in October is a fine placeholder.

Doug's Knob, October, Nachusa Grasslands, Illinois, October 20, 2017, Oil on canvas, 18 x 26 in.

The first quiet minutes of sunlight on a December morning reveal the rocky substrate that saved Doug's Knob from the plow. The accompanying boulders, dumped here at the base of the knob, would have been unwelcome in the cornfield that ran up to this point. Although every dormant stem of grass and lingering oak leaf glowed with an intensely warm light, my fingers were too numb to get far with painting that morning. I finished this one in the studio.

Doug's Knob, December, Nachusa Grasslands, Illinois, December 18, 2018, Oil on canvas, 18 x 26 in.

Nachusa Bison, Nachusa Grasslands, Illinois, 2021, Oil on canvas, 24 x 36 in.

Bison were integral to the ecology of the historic tallgrass prairie. One transformative effect they had was observed by a Jesuit chronicler near the Illinois and Kankakee Rivers.

In this Route we see only vast Meadows, with little clusters of Trees here and there, which seem to have been planted by the Hand; the Grass grows so high in them, that one might lose one's self amongst it; but every where we meet with Paths that are as beaten as they can be in the most populous Countries; yet nothing passes through them but Buffaloes, and from Time to Time some Herds of Dear, and some Roe-Bucks.

–Pierre-François-Xavier de Charlevoix, *Letters to the Dutchess of Lesdiguiéres,* from the English translation published in 1763

On my first visit to Nachusa Grasslands in 2015, when I needed to go off trail in search of painting perspectives, I generally met with a dense and continuous cover of restored grasses and forbs. But on subsequent visits, with my favorite subject areas now enclosed by Nachusa's bison fence, I frequently found "beaten paths" to follow, and prairie cover becoming more diversified in its physical structure—perhaps like that seen by early explorers. As they did in the historic tallgrass prairie, bison now play an important role as environmental engineers at Nachusa, creating niches for a wider variety of prairie plants and animals that thrive where the bison tramp, wallow, and graze.

As I was on my way to Doug's Knob to start my December study there (p. 75), I was treated to this frosty view of a few young bulls.

Oak Island, Nachusa Grasslands, Illinois, June 12, 2018, Oil on canvas, 8 x 16 in.

Absent for two centuries, bison can again be seen in Illinois performing their conservation duties (and adding interest to the landscape) at the U.S. Forest Service's Midewin National Tallgrass Prairie and at Nachusa Grasslands. They can also be seen next door at the Indiana Nature Conservancy's 8,400-acre Kankakee Sands Preserve. I missed them at Midewin but have had the pleasure of working among them, with caution, several times at Nachusa, where their 2014 reintroduction is already showing signs of diversifying habitats. With any luck, it will facilitate the return of the upland sandpiper, a grassland bird that prefers the low vegetation

Rest Area, Kankakee Sands Preserve, Indiana, May 14, 2019, Oil on canvas, 8 x 16 in.

height the bison create; its call was what first alerted Doug and Dot Wade to the prairie remnants of Nachusa. The Kankakee Sands bison are performing similar duties, improving plant diversity for grassland birds with their grazing and creating habitat for amphibians and other animals in their wallows. While Nachusa's herd kept me on my toes when I painted in their territory, Indiana's presented me a chance for a closer study, resting as they were just beyond the preserve's fence.

Frequent, widespread fires caused by humans and lightning prevented the presettlement tallgrass prairie from transitioning to forest. Today, prescribed burning maintains the ecological integrity at Nachusa Grasslands and other prairie preserves. It is both a sublime phenomenon to observe and an exciting challenge to paint, requiring a bit more preparation than my other subjects. I ensure my safety by staying current on my wildland firefighter training and maintaining a good rapport with the burn crew.

With the permission and guidance of The Nature Conservancy's Bill Kleiman, I tagged along with Nachusa's fire crew on several burns during the 2018–2019 burn season, exploring the aesthetics of prairie fire through field painting. By focusing on the atmospheric effects of flame and smoke in the prairie's dormant season, I was able to capture something of the compelling aesthetic experience known to prescribed fire practitioners. Due to the dynamic nature of the subjects, all the paintings were done very quickly, with brushstrokes more gestural than I usually employ. That was particularly true of the several small studies made close to the flame front. There was less urgency when the front was at a distance, but even distant smoke plumes (right), changed rapidly. By the time I started a second painting on this location, *Receding Flame Front* (p. 87), the foreground had been entirely transformed.

Two paintings that were completed one right after the other, *Flame Front Arriving* (p. 82) and *Flame Front Departing* (p. 83), illustrate one of my favorite field painting experiences. First, I worked from the "green," staying about a hundred feet ahead of the wind-driven flame front, with all my gear on my back or on the easel. Then, after stepping over the diminished flames when the wind dropped (wearing fire-resistant boots and Nomex clothing), I switched canvases and painted from the smoldering "black," following behind the flames. I moved my easel about a dozen times over a few hundred yards to finish both paintings. A small dirt road served as a handy escape route should I have needed it, a constant consideration when working a prescribed burn.

All of the works in this series (pp. 81–87) are oil on canvas and a few include ashes that were trapped in the wet paint before they were finished.

Smoke Plumes, Nachusa Grasslands, Illinois, March 26, 2019, Oil on canvas, 12 x 16 in.

Flame Front Arriving, Nachusa Grasslands, Illinois, March 23, 2019, Oil on canvas, 9 x 11 in.

Flame Front Departing, Nachusa Grasslands, Illinois, March 23, 2019, Oil on canvas, 9 x 12 in.

Winter Burn 1, Nachusa Grasslands, Illinois, December 18, 2018, 9 x 12 in.

Winter Burn 2, Nachusa Grasslands, Illinois, December 18, 2018, 9 x 12 in.

Backing Uphill, Nachusa Grasslands, Illinois, March 23, 2019, 9 x 12 in.

Building Black, Nachusa Grasslands, Illinois, March 25, 2019, 9 x 12 in.

Fall Burn 1, Nachusa Grasslands, Illinois, November 15, 2018, 9 x 12 in.

Fall Burn 2, Nachusa Grasslands, Illinois, November 15, 2018, 9 x 11 in.

Smoke Columns, Nachusa Grasslands, Illinois, March 25, 2019, 9 x 12 in.

Fall Burn 3, Nachusa Grasslands, Illinois, November 15, 2018, 9 x 11 in.

Combustion, Nachusa Grasslands, Illinois, March 26, 2019, Oil on canvas, 9 x 12 in.

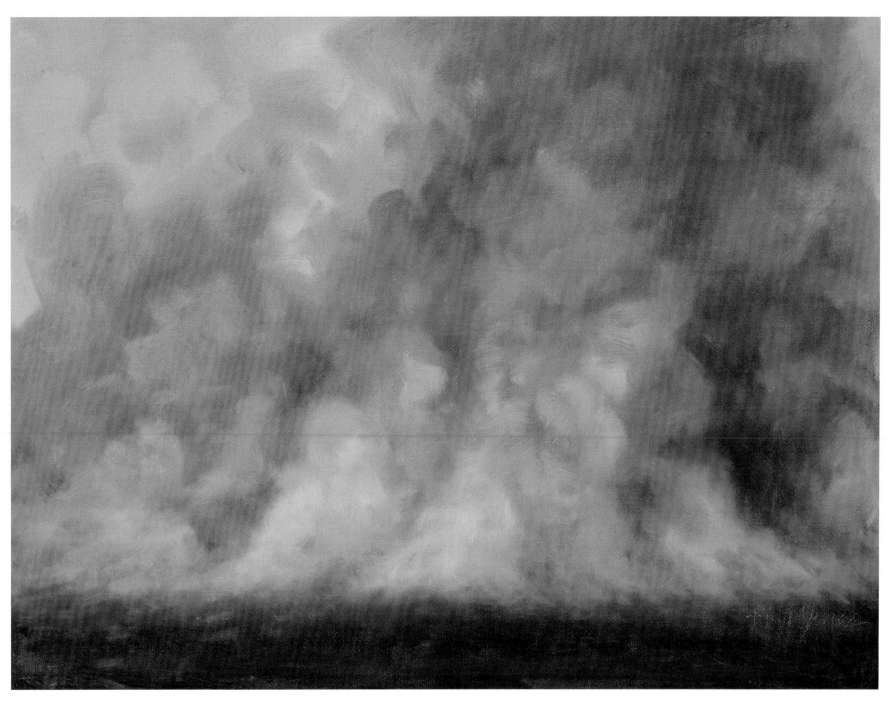

Receding Flame Front, Nachusa Grasslands, Illinois, March 26, 2019, Oil on canvas, 9 x 12 in.

Beaver Pond, Nachusa Grasslands, Illinois, 2019, Oil on canvas, 30 x 54 in.

Late afternoon sunlight on fire-managed prairie grasses and floating mats of duckweed made a striking contrast with darkening skies above this Nachusa beaver pond. Besides creating an ideal September setting for a landscape painter, the beavers impounding Wade Creek are increasing biodiversity in the preserve with new habitat for wetland plants and animals. Widespread before European settlement, beavers were virtually extirpated from Illinois a century ago, but following reintroduction programs in the 1930s they have returned to every county in the state.

Flint Creek Savanna, Lake County, Illinois, 2020, Oil on canvas, 24 x 40 in.

Frozen hard in February, the solid surface of this little prairie wetland made it easy for me to frame an enticing view toward the beautiful old oak groves across Flint Creek. Decades earlier, with well-drained cropland on this spot, I would have had no such luck. Barrington-based Citizens for Conservation, a volunteer group that purchased and began restoring this site thirty-two years ago, broke the agricultural drain tiles beneath this low spot and restored its natural hydrology and associated native wetland species. It is one of a mosaic of high-quality prairie environments they have beautifully restored along Flint Creek.

In all three of the following field paintings (pp. 91–93), I was attracted to watery surfaces reflecting the mood of the passing weather. Each site is a state nature preserve, identified many decades ago as an important resource to preserve for future generations. They offered me a chance to see tallgrass prairie remnants at the wetter end of the spectrum.

Of the three, Lockport Prairie Preserve is perhaps the most unusual. It's a small remnant of a unique prairie type that occurred on thin soils over dolomitic limestone bedrock, mainly in the Des Plaines River floodplain. A high water table and unusual soil properties create a variety of wet-to-dry habitats that support both common and uncommon species. The preserve is owned and managed (with much help from volunteers) by the Forest Preserve District of Will County. At one point it was considered as a spoils dump for an expansion of the nearby Chicago Sanitary and Ship Canal. Now under Illinois Nature Preserves protection, its greatest threats are invasive plants and altered hydrology. In this view, with a thunderstorm as a backdrop, gradations of color denote habitat transitions across the floodplain. I took some artistic license to extend the prairie up the bank of the bluff, as I imagine it might have looked in the past.

Lockport Prairie, Will County, Illinois, June 15, 2018, Oil on canvas, 9 x 11 in.

Wet Prairie, Goose Lake Prairie State Natural Area, Illinois, June 14, 2018, Oil on canvas, 9 x 11 in.

Due to its flatness and the robust prairie grasses that can obscure the view, it's hard to appreciate the scale and configuration of Goose Lake Prairie, an Illinois Nature Preserve located below the confluence of the Des Plaines and Kankakee Rivers. Established in 1969, it is the largest tallgrass prairie remnant in Illinois. However, from the observation deck at the visitor's center (a luxury of elevation the early settlers didn't have), I could better appreciate the mosaic of wet-to-mesic prairie communities that hold more than 400 species in these 1,500-plus acres.

Spring Lake Wetland, Cook County, Illinois, May 13, 2019, Oil on canvas, 9 x 12 in.

A warmly streaked morning overcast compelled me to pull over and quickly set up my painting box at the edge of Spring Lake Nature Preserve in the northwest corner of Cook County. At the roadside, where the dormant vegetation had been recently burned off, spring green-up was most pronounced, but in the distance a swath of unburned beige cattails delineated the marshes around Spring and Mud Lakes. I would enjoy further teasing out the relationship between this foreground marsh and those of the lakes as I later worked on a larger presettlement view of the scene.

I could but think what a view for a painter of landscapes, the marsh extending as far as the eye could see, covered with the thick high grass, and the little cluster of tall and bright green tamaracks in the center, and the marsh surrounded by groves of oak extending on here and there. Altogether the view was most splendid and far beyond the powers of a painter to describe.

—Colbee Benton, *A Visitor to Chicago in Indian Days: "Journal to the 'Far-Off West.'"* 1833

Presettlement Marsh Study, 2020, Oil on canvas, 8 x 12 in.

In studying the Illinois prairie, I have often wondered what the vast wetlands described by early travelers were like. Colbee Benton's description of an unspoiled marsh "extending as far as the eye could see" resonated with me—as did his challenge to paint one. His "splendid view" in today's Lake County is only twenty miles from a lovely, but much smaller, marsh I had earlier photographed and painted (p. 93). After first composing a small study (below left) to conceptualize Colbee's description, I assembled my observations into a larger canvas that recreates the view from Bateman Road, picturing the state nature preserve and a wide view of Spring Creek valley as it might have appeared in Benton's time. In the distance, presettlement oak groves cover morainal hills with interludes of prairie, and in the foreground is an assemblage of species based on those found there today, including common water plantain, wild mint, river bulrush, narrow-leaved cattail, water pepper, and swamp milkweed.

Spring Creek Valley c. 1833, Spring Lake Preserve, Illinois, 2020, Oil on canvas, 24 x 36 in.

Late Afternoon on the Grand Prairie of Illinois c. 1491, 2019, Oil on canvas, 36 x 60 in.

It's interesting to consider that today's Illinois farmland and the state's historic prairies are both cultural landscapes; one shaped by modern machinery, the other a relic of frequent burning by Native Americans. But when gazing across the endless corn and soybean fields, farmsteads, and tree lines of today's Grand Prairie, it's hard to imagine the prairie the original inhabitants knew. European travelers who saw Illinois' presettlement prairies often relied on analogies to the open ocean, for lack of comparable landscape references, to convey what it was like to experience them. While many of those accounts celebrated the magnificence of the scenery, some were tinged with a sense of isolation and insignificance on the part of the viewer. Such was the sentiment of Caleb Atwater crossing the northern part of the state.

Sometimes I traveled, during four or five hours, either by day or by night, across some prairie, without seeing even a bush, or a tree–above me, were the wide spread and lofty heavens, while the prairie, with its grasses and flowers, extended in all directions around me, far beyond the reach of my vision. In such a situation, man feels his own littleness, in the immensity of space, he feels alone too, in this loneliness, universal silence and repose.

–Caleb Atwater, *Remarks Made on a Tour to Prairie du Chien*, 1831

Such descriptions motivated me to picture what that experience was like before Europeans arrived, the prairie devoid of today's "improvements." The resulting composition is based on prairie topography north of Champaign, floral observations from various remnant black-soil prairies, and atmospheric observations from across the state.

In the presettlement tallgrass prairie, wildfires, particularly at night, stretching across miles of unbroken prairie, were often described as both terrifying and beautiful by those who witnessed them.

A wildfire on the prairie was a magnificent spectacle, combining all the elements of terror and grandeur. It compared with a fire in the woods or in a city as Niagara compares with the waterfall of a mill-dam.

–David Turpie,
Sketches of My Own Times, 1903

No sight can be more sublime, than to behold at night, a stream of fire several miles in breadth, advancing across these plains, leaving behind it a black cloud of smoke, and throwing before it a vivid glare which lights up the whole landscape with the brilliancy of noonday.

–James Hall,
Notes on The Western States, 1838

I imagine such spectacles were observed countless times before they awed European arrivals. In this scene, a companion to *Late Afternoon on the Grand Prairie of Illinois, c. 1491*, a horizon-spanning prairie fire, still over a mile away, casts an otherworldly glow, while above it stars appear at the fading of twilight. At this distance, I imagine the roar of the flame front is barely audible, like the sound of waves when you are still far enough from the seashore, although a sense of impending danger should be apparent in the unbroken cover of grasses (fuel) that extends across the foreground. Large prairie fires were, however, not a great danger to the traveler, as the flame front could be crossed easily in sections where it was diminished, but they were a threat to early settlements and were soon extinguished, along with the prairie they sustained.

With so little left of the Illinois prairie, it's wonderful to see those fires rekindled in recent decades, albeit much smaller and now highly controlled, by people who have recognized the importance of tallgrass prairie ecology. Their restoration efforts are allowing prairie species to flourish again and give all of us a chance to get to know this rare, beautiful, and quintessentially American ecosystem.

Night Fire on the Grand Prairie of Illinois c. 1491, 2019, Oil on canvas, 36 x 60 in.

Locations Painted

Poplar Creek Prairie, Cook County, Illinois, July 25, 2013, Oil on paper, 7.5 x 7.5 in.

Note: Locations with "Nature Preserve" in the title are part of the Illinois Nature Preserves System.

12. **Nachusa Grasslands**. The Nature Conservancy. Near Franklin Grove, Illinois. Pages 43, 44, 62–78, and 81–88.

13. **Foley Sand Prairie Nature Preserve**. Illinois Department of Natural Resources. In Lee County near Deer Grove, Illinois. Pages 46 and 47.

14. **Hanover Bluff Nature Preserve**. Illinois Department of Natural Resources. Near Hanover, Jo Davies County, Illinois. Page 53.

15. **Kankakee Sands Preserve**. The Nature Conservancy. Near Morocco, Newton County, Indiana. Page 79.

16. **Pembroke Savanna Nature Preserve**. The Nature Conservancy. Near Hopkins Park, Illinois. Page 55.

17. **Loda Cemetery Prairie Nature Preserve**. Grand Prairie Friends. Loda, Illinois. Page 39.

18. **Prospect Cemetery Prairie Nature Preserve**. Illinois Department of Natural Resources. Paxton, Illinois. Page 38.

19. **Revis Hill Prairie Nature Preserve**. Illinois Department of Natural Resources. Near Kilbourne, Mason County, Illinois. Page 52.

20. **Sand Prairie-Scrub Oak Nature Preserve**. Illinois Department of Natural Resources. Near Bath, Mason County, Illinois. Page 48.

21. **Fults Hill Prairie Nature Preserve**. Illinois Department of Natural Resources. In Monroe County near Prairie Du Roche, Illinois. Page 51.

22. **Cave Creek Glade Nature Preserve**. Illinois Department of Natural Resources. Near Vienna in Johnson County, Illinois. Page 56.

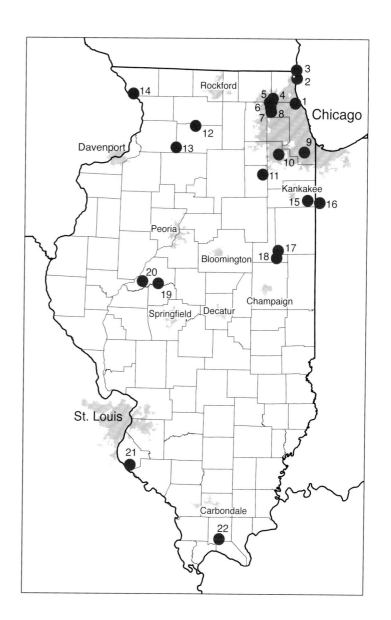

List of Paintings

Acknowledgments

This book and its corresponding exhibit at the Chicago Botanic Garden would not have made it into the world without a lot of help.

First, I am immensely grateful to Hank and Wendy Paulson. From Wendy's introducing me to local prairie ecology and ecologists, to Hank's generous foreword for this book, their encouragement, advice, and hospitality were the kernel around which the rest of this undertaking grew.

As the project expanded, so did my need to understand the ecological function of the various sites I was portraying and why they looked the way they did. I am forever grateful to Laurel Ross, Randy Nyboer, Bill Kleiman, Stephen Packard, and the late Tom Vanderpoel for sharing their ecological and restoration expertise with me, bringing much greater depth to these images. I am especially grateful to Stephen for his essay, which gives context to this body of work and how it relates to the culture of conservation that all of these extraordinary people embody.

Early in the project, I had the great fortune to get to know Jerry Adelmann of Openlands. I thank him for encouraging me to put this book together, and for his efforts, and those of his staff, on behalf of the exhibition. In addition to Jerry, I thank Michelle Carr and Ken Modzelewski of The Nature Conservancy; Arnold Randall and Cathy Geraghty of the Forest Preserves of Cook County; Jean M. Franczyk and Jennifer Schwarz Ballard of the Chicago Botanic Garden; Laurel Ross and Debra Moskovits of the Field Museum; and Susan Willets, Wendy Paulson, and Justin Pepper for their ideas and work to ensure that the exhibition's conservation message could be brought to as wide an audience as possible.

I feel deeply honored to have been invited to exhibit at the Chicago Botanic Garden. *Picturing the Prairie* was originally scheduled for 2020, but after COVID-19 shut everything down it was, thankfully, postponed for a year. I thank all of the wonderful staff I've had the pleasure to meet at the Garden for their work in preparing to host the exhibition in spite of pandemic challenges. I'm especially grateful to Gabriel Hutchison and Nancy Snyder for designing the exhibit—and for generously including me in that process—and for then redesigning it to accommodate social distancing requirements. I would also like to thank the team from the Field Museum who together with the Chicago Botanic Garden prepared a series of field guides to the flora depicted in six of the paintings in the exhibit.

For kindly reviewing or proofreading various portions of this book, I thank Laurie Anderson, Dorinda Dallmeyer, Susan Kleiman, Randy Nyboer, Stephen Packard, Justin Pepper, and Abby Sterling. Justin and Dorinda's counsel throughout the project was especially helpful. I was fortunate to have Janice Shay of Pinafore Press design this book; she is an artist in her own right. I thank her and editor John Harris for improving the clarity of this manuscript, and Brad Sanders for creating the maps.

I am grateful to the Bobolink Foundation for supporting this publication, and for all they do to promote conservation.

I would never have been able to experience (let alone share a vision of) the tallgrass ecosystem without the dedicated individuals and organizations that preserve, restore, and maintain what little of it remains. I am especially grateful to the Illinois Department of Natural Resources—which is to say, the people of Illinois—and its Nature Preserves System, The Nature Conservancy in Illinois (especially its Nachusa staff), Friends of Nachusa Grasslands, Forest Preserves of Cook County, Poplar Creek Prairie Stewards, and Citizens for Conservation. Most of the places represented in this book are under their care. For their stewardship of the many other sites I visited and/or painted, I thank the National Park Service; the United States Forest Service; the Wisconsin and Indiana Departments of Natural Resources; the Forest Preserve Districts of Byron County, DuPage County, Kane County, McHenry County, and Will County; the Wisconsin and Indiana chapters of The Nature Conservancy; Grand Prairie Friends; Friends of Lockport Prairie; the Natural Land Institute; the Illinois Audubon Society; Northeastern Illinois University; Munson Township, Illinois; Paxton Township Cemetery Association; private landowners of preserves; and all of the individuals and groups that work with them. This book and the paintings within celebrate their achievements.

Finally, my wife Beth Gavrilles has supported me throughout every aspect of this project, from critiquing painting compositions and rooting out the excessive use of adjectives in my writing, to simply keeping me going. She has, as ever, my eternal gratitude and love.

Author/Contributors

Philip Juras is a landscape painter whose work is an expression of his desire to explore, understand, and conserve healthy natural environments. He combines direct observation with the study of natural science and history to depict, and in some cases recreate, these landscapes in oil on canvas. His 2011 exhibition *The Southern Frontier, Landscapes Inspired by Bartram's "Travels"* at the Telfair Museums in Savannah and the Morris Museum of Art in Augusta, Georgia, portrayed the southern wilderness as William Bartram described it in the 1770s. *The Wild Treasury of Nature, A Portrait of Little St. Simons Island*, his 2016 exhibition at the Morris Museum and the Marietta Cobb Museum in Marietta, Georgia, examined the natural environments of one of the East Coast's most ecologically intact barrier islands. In 2017 he exhibited *Landscapes of Chingaza (Paisajes de Chingaza)* at the Biblioteca Virgilio Barco in Bogotá, Colombia, celebrating the high elevation environments of Colombia's Chingaza National Park. He is the author of *The Southern Frontier*, published by the Telfair Museums in 2011, for which he was named Georgia Author of the Year in the Specialty Book category by the Georgia Writers Association, and *The Wild Treasury of Nature*, published by the University of Georgia Press in 2016. Juras also volunteers as a wildland firefighter, or "ecoburner," with the Georgia Department of Natural Resources and The Nature Conservancy. He holds degrees in landscape architecture and fine arts from the University of Georgia.

Stephen Packard has for decades worked to develop the practice and popular understanding of ecological restoration and biodiversity conservation. He has served as field representative for the Illinois Nature Preserves Commission, director of Science and Stewardship with The Nature Conservancy in Illinois, and founding director of Audubon Chicago Region. He started the Volunteer Stewardship Network, which became a model for similar projects across the U.S. and internationally. He was the primary founder of the Chicago Region Biodiversity Council ("Chicago Wilderness"), a globally respected collaboration of more than 200 national and local agencies that helped establish biodiversity conservation as a core part of the region's culture. He initiated and helped design and implement many of Illinois' larger ecological restoration projects at Nachusa Grasslands and the Poplar Creek, Orland Grassland, and Spring Creek Forest Preserves. He helped found the Society for Ecological Restoration, which now has chapters throughout the world. He is the editor, with Cornelia Mutel, of *The Tallgrass Restoration Handbook* and has taught conservation at Northwestern University. He currently works with a variety of efforts to conserve wildlife and habitat and "create a culture of conservation" through which people and nature can re-establish mutually nourishing relationships in a changing world.

Henry M. Paulson, Jr., is a businessman, China expert, conservationist, and author. He is the founder and chairman of the Paulson Institute, a "think and do" tank that aims to strengthen the economic and environmental relationship between the U.S. and China. Paulson served as the seventy-fourth secretary of the Treasury from July 2006 to January 2009. Prior to that, he had a thirty-two year career at Goldman Sachs, serving as chairman and Chief Executive Officer beginning in 1999. A lifelong conservationist, Paulson has served as chairman of The Peregrine Fund and of The Nature Conservancy Global Board of Directors. He founded and co-chaired the Conservancy's Asia-Pacific Council and Latin American Conservation Council. He has written four books, including the best-selling *On the Brink*, in which he details his experiences as Treasury secretary fending off the near-collapse of the U.S. economy during the Great Recession, and *Dealing with China*; both have been translated into multiple languages. He and his wife, nature educator Wendy Paulson, live adjacent to a remnant hillside prairie and have been active in grassland restoration for many years.

Works Cited

Atwater, Caleb. *Remarks made on a tour to Prairie du Chien; thence to Washington City, in 1829.* Columbus: Isaac N. Whiting, 1831.
https://archive.org/details/remarksmadeontou00atwa

Benton, Colbee. *A Visitor to Chicago in Indian Days: "Journal to the 'Far-Off West.'"* 1833, ed. Paul M. Angle and James R. Getz. Chicago: Caxton Club, 1957, reprinted in *Prairie, Woods, and Water: Two Centuries of Chicago Nature Writing,* ed. Joel Greenberg, Chicago: University of Chicago Press, 2008.

Betz, Robert F. *The Prairie of the Illinois Country.* Westmont, Ill.: DPM Ink, 2011.

Betz, Robert F. "What is a Prairie?" In *The Prairie: Swell and Swale, From Nature.* by Torkel Korling. Dundee, Ill.: Torkel Korling, 1972.

Charlevoix, Pierre-Francois-Xavier. "Letter XXVI," in *Letters to the Dutchess of Lesdiguiéres; Giving an Account of a Voyage to Canada, and Travels through that Country, and Louisiana, to the Gulf of Mexico.* London: Goadby, 1763.
https://archive.org/details/letterstodutches00char

Illinois Nature Preserves Commission. *2015-2020 Strategic Plan with Implementation Objectives: Public Review Draft.*
https://www2.illinois.gov/dnr/INPC/Documents/INPC15_20Strat PlanPublicReviewDraft81115.pdf

Hall, James. *Notes on The Western States; Containing Descriptive Sketches of Their Soil, Climate, Resources and Scenery.* Philadelphia: Harrison Hall, 1838.
https://archive.org/details/notesonwesterns00hallgoog

Husar, John. "Forest Preserve Restoration Comes From 'Outside' Help," *Chicago Tribune,* (Chicago, Illinois), June 18, 1989.
https://www.chicagotribune.com/news/ct-xpm-1989-06-18-8902100795-story.html

Kinsey, Joni L. *Plain Pictures, Images of the American Prairie.* Washington: Smithsonian Institution Press, 1996.

Leopold, Aldo. *A Sand County Almanac: With Essays on Conservation from Round River.* New York: Ballantine Books, 1991.

Noss, Reed. *Forgotten Grasslands of the South: Natural History and Conservation.* Washington: Island Press, 2013.

Thoreau, Henry David. *The Writings of Henry David Thoreau: Journal. Vol. XI, July 2, 1858-February 28, 1859,* ed. Bradford Torrey. Boston: Houghton Mifflin, 1906.
https://www.walden.org/wp-content/uploads/2016/02/Journal-11-Chapter-4.pdf

Turpie, David. *Sketches of My Own Times.* Indianapolis: The Bobbs-Merrill Company, 1903.
https://archive.org/details/sketchesofmyownts00turp

Watts, May T. Handwritten letter to Barbara Turner, December 11, 1958. Photocopy given by Turner to Stephen Packard.

Wilhelm, Gerould and Laura Rericha, *Flora of the Chicago Region.* Indianapolis: Indiana Academy of Science, 2017.

Wilson, Edward O. *Biophilia.* Cambridge, Mass.: Harvard University Press, 2009.